HOW F?
[The Q

To: Gracie!
From: Marc
'the flower'

To: Grace!
From: Marc
Get Well Soon!

M

HOW HIGH DO YOU WANNA FLY?

[The Quest for Sustainable Personal Growth]

MARK GUEVARA

Digital Artery Media Group Publishing, Tampa, FL

No part of this book may be reproduced, stored in a retrieval system, or transmitted in any form or by any means—electronic, mechanical, photocopy, recording, or otherwise—except for brief quotations for the purpose of review or comment, without the prior permission of the publisher, Digital Artery Media Group Publishing, Tampa, FL 33511

Copyright © 2012 by Mark Guevara

All rights reserved.

Published in the United States by Digital Artery Media Group Publishing, Tampa, FL

Library of Congress Cataloguing-in-Publication Data
Guevara, Mark
how high do you wanna fly? [The Quest for Personal Sustainable Growth]
p. cm
ISBN 978-0-9844016-2-8 (lk paper) ISBN 978-0-9844016-3-5 (ebook)
1. How High 2. Social Change 3. Personal Growth

Printed in the United States of America on acid-free paper

www.damgrp.com/markguevara

Book design by dArtery

To Beverly, Seth-Marq and Ysatis Elizabeth, and, to my nephew Carver whose indefatigable courage and raw determination to succeed has served as a template of inspiration to our family; and, to those to whom persistent growth is an intentional, deliberate pursuit…

CONTENTS

ACKNOWLEDGEMENTS

INTRODUCTION

1. **PURSUING PERSONAL CHANGE:**   15
   How We Pursue Change
   Whatever discontent you can and are willing to tolerate and ignore, you are unwilling and unable to address...
   MARK GUEVARA

2. **PURSUING SUSTAINABLE PERSONAL GROWTH:**   28
   How We Continue Changing
   It is the capacity to develop and improve your skills that distinguishes leaders from followers.
   BENNIS AND NANUS

3. **MOVEMENT IN CHANGE AND GROWTH:**   35
   What Promotes Change.
   There can be no change without movement.
   MARK GUEVARA.

4. **THE FLIGHT METAPHOR:**   41
   Relating Flight to the Growth Process.
   Flight and growth are both multi-dimensional. Just as flight is not simply upward elevation, so personal growth is not just intellectual ascent.
   MARK GUEVARA

5. **EAGLE OR JET?**   46
   How High Do You Want to Fly?
   The heights by great men reached and kept, were not obtained by sudden flight, but they, while their companions slept, were toiling upward in the night.
   HENRY WADSWORTH LONGFELLOW

6. HOW HIGH CAN YOU FLY? 52
   The Role of Your Desire
   Your personal drive and efficiency as a human being is intricately interwoven in your own ability to do and be.
   FRANCES HESSELBEIN

7. THE ROLE OF KNOWLEDGE IN PERSONAL GROWTH: 63
   How Knowledge Makes You a Better Decision Maker.
   If you know the enemy and know yourself, you need not fear the result of a hundred battles.
   SUN TZU

8. IMPEDIMENTS TO FLIGHT: 69
   Dealing With Obstacles.
   Obstacles are opportunities to solve problems...
   MARK GUEVARA

9. THE IMPORTANCE OF FLIGHT INSTRUCTORS: 88
   The Role of Mentors.
   You cannot learn to fly by yourself...
   MARK GUEVARA

10. DISCIPLINE: 94
    Where Growth Becomes a Sustainable Habit
    The one who loves discipline loves knowledge, but the one who hates reproof is stupid.
    PROVERBS 12:1

❖ ACKNOWLEDGEMENTS ❖

My wife has been the pillar of encouragement and an unfailing object of inspiration to me. Our children have served to constantly keep me focused on what really matters as we positioned them to navigate this world. This book could not have been written if there was not a personal discontentment with my own life. Period. Admittedly, I have read many leadership and personal productivity books from which I synthesized, distilled and culled some of the useful principles that have helped me change, grow and refine the process all over again. However, the majority of this book's content is original thinking.

INTRODUCTION

Where are you, where do you want to go and how are you going to get there? This book explores those questions and provides a framework for thoughtful introspection by focusing on change principles that promote personal effectiveness and at the same time using the three pillar principles of *evaluation*, *movement* and *destination*. By focusing on evaluation, movement and destination as they relate to personal growth, the author utilizes the metaphor of flight and relates them to *where you are, where do you want to go and how you expect to eventually get there respectively*. Additionally, *who you are, who you want to become, and how you eventually become* is another way of looking at the three pillars. It was written on the basic premise that every well-meaning individual wants to achieve their best, they desire growth and personal effectiveness. Growth and personal effectiveness however, whether you choose to believe it or not to, are profoundly and intentionally spiritual.

In the spring of 2003, (the exact date eludes me), I just happened to flip the cable channel to CNN. Larry King was interviewing Stedman Graham (the permanent fiancé of Oprah Winfrey). I had seen Stedman a number of years ago when I worked for a major publisher in New York City. He was always however, confidently poised and affable. I had never heard him speak so I wanted to hear how he was going to respond to Larry King's questions. He was brilliant! He talked about his commitment to education and his personal branding philosophy and gave a few plugs for books he had written (which I highly recommend). He also made some significant statements about personal effectiveness that caught my attention. During the course of his interview, he said something that left an ineradicable mark upon my mind. He said, "Everyone of us has twenty-four hours at our disposal and how effective we are in maximizing that time, can have a significant impact on the direction of our lives (paraphrased)." I have thought a lot about what he said. In fact, I decided to take action on what he said. (Thank you Stedman). That was a turning point in my life. That night, I went to bed thinking about what he said. When I awoke the next morning, I got an idea to change the way I was handling my time. I will share this with you later on.

I believe that human beings are tridimensional in nature, to borrow a phrase from some preachers. We have emotions, a will and an intellect. We also have a body, mind and spirit. Growth therefore has to be tridimensional as well to fully exploit its far reaching results. In my personal life, I have asked myself many, many questions. However, the most agonizing one that I have ever asked myself and some of my closest associates, has been this one probing and life-changing question—How far do you want to go with your life? How High Do You Want To Fly? What can you do to improve and continue to improve your own personal effectiveness? Have I done all that there is to be done to be a more effective human being, to move beyond my current personal productivity engine, and to be more consistent in my growth efforts. What can I do to move beyond using ten percent of my brain as the average human rarely does. What does it take to achieve sustainable change and growth?

As I write this book, I hope I will answer those questions for you. These questions are important because real personal growth should be a constant and perpetual quest. In order for us to have meaningful and fruitful lives, our goals must be to live lives that will bear the fruits of effectiveness that influence the lives of others. I hope you do. We must reach beyond our own personal struggles and forge in our mental crucible the kind of individual who is capable of constant change. As iron sharpens iron, so I believe that we will attract other individuals who desire a different kind of existence that is way beyond what they are currently experiencing. I am sure by now you would have deducted that this book is about personal growth and personal change.

Before we can grow, we must want to grow, there has to be that personal defining catalyst called *desire* that pushes and drives us to grow and change. There must be a deliberate personal discontent or dissatisfaction with the present trajectory of your life. One of my friends Dr. E.L.Kersten calls this conditon *Despair*. The posture and attitude of our hearts must be ones of profound personal dissatisfaction with our own status quo. There has to be that cry in your heart for change. You must do a serious and probing evaluation to identify that place of inner discontent with the way your life is going and start moving until you start seeing meaningful change. You must make a volitional choice for the kind of life you want to live and chart a different course to achieve it. *There can be no change without movement.* This is a fundamental law. That is how change takes place. Invariably also, there can be no growth without change as the nature of growth is evolutionary. We will embark on this journey together and find that place, define that catalyst, discover that stimulant that will move us from place to place and set in motion the drivers that enable us to grow, achieve sustainable growth and meaningful outcomes.

Mark Guevara

How High Do You Wanna Fly?

PART ONE

EVALUATION ESSENTIALS

1

PURSUING PERSONAL CHANGE:

How we pursue change

Whatever discontent you can and are willing to tolerate and ignore, you are unwilling and unable to address...
MARK GUEVARA

In 2001, I was sitting at the foot of the bed reading a law textbook while my wife was going over some of the material she had been exposed to during a manager's meeting. Her eyes fell upon a line that was written in Dr. Covey's book " The 7 Highly Effective Habits for Managers." What she read was a quote by Albert Einstein, which read, "The significant problems we face cannot be solved at the same level of thinking we were as when they were created". We all react differently to things that strike a distinctive chord within us. When she read that, I frankly had never read that line from Einstein before, so I rose up from where I was sitting and asked her to read it again. She did.

That was a *kairos*[1] revelatory moment for me. That was another defining moment for me! There was such a powerful principle hidden in those lines that had immense spiritual implications for me. Albert Einstein arguably, was one of the greatest minds of our time. If you read the story of the life of Albert Einstein, you will discover that he was not born a genius. He was not excessively intelligent. In fact, he was an awkward individual growing up in Germany at the time. The competitive world we live in today sometimes make us feel that genius is a birthright. It is not. Einstein was a slow learner.[2] Surprised! Not really. There are individuals who by virtue of a desire to overcome some personal handicap, or some weakness, who push themselves way beyond their known personal limits. Their own handicaps serve as catalysts to empower them to a higher place of purpose and performance. I did some

---

1 kairos

2 The Life of Einstein

research on the reservoir from which that powerful principle emanated and discovered that Einstein was constantly seeking to find answers to the meaning of life and its existence and to the meaning of the universe. His EMC2 theory was resultant after many, many long hours of probing and questioning. His mind was used to the constant exercise of reasoning, of questioning and problem-solving pursuits, the words significant problems have weighted meaning. Solving the problem of the relativity of matter is no easy problem.

The problems or situations in your life must be ones that bring you to frequent moments of discontent. Discontent for the intents and purposes of this book are those elements in your life that you just cannot live with and some you cannot live without. It could be a bad vice, spousal abuse, desires to achieve something that you have struggled with all your life. These are things that if you do not address them they will ruin your chances of performing better, achieving a goal or worse, take you to an early grave. These things must stir you up and compel you to want or desire change. How deep does your well of desire go? They must leave you with sleepless nights sometimes.

Additionally, the problem or problems have

to be construed as meaning something to solve, a situational dilemma, a process to innovate, a debilitating habit to conquer or a generational vice to overcome or a business problem to solve.

The real problem lies in the fact that many of us are contented with where we are. There is a blinding almost debilitating situational opiate that leaves us contented with where we are. I hate to use this rather crude analogy but it will suffice for now. If you love a man or a woman and they are abusive, (by the way abuse comes in many forms), there is something almost mystical about a relationship between a man and a woman that sometimes makes us feel that it is taboo if we try to address abuse. If your spouse is abusive, it is wrong and you have no rhyme nor reason enduring or tolerating that kind of punishment. I know taking the first step is difficult. This is a level two problem and you are at level one. I once heard a South African speaker[31] say that we cannot solve level two problems with level one thinking and I got excited when I heard that because he had quoted Albert Einstein. If the problem is higher than you are emotionally able to handle get help from a source that can handle that level of problem.

Level two problems are significant and have the capability to bring your life and the life of others into a whole new debilitating dimension, or it could potentially ruin your business. If it has the potential to change you, it is really big, if it has the potential to radically change and influence the lives of others, it is significant. In Webster's dictionary surprisingly, the definition for significant that got my attention is the second one that says, "having or likely to have influence or effect."

Before you dismiss this as humanistic musings to understand change please understand that I believe that all truth comes from God. Period. Regardless of whom he uses to dispense it. The significant problem that you are facing whether it is a weakness that you have tried to overcome, an indulgence that you have tried to hide because you just cannot conquer it, or a business problem you keep having to face over and over again.

When I was a young man, there were many things that I struggled with until I began to understand who I was and what my true potential was. As I began to mature, I struggled less with other areas that had the potential to ruin my personal destiny, but I gained a greater understanding of who I was. This is where I began to understand the principle of change. Before you can go to level two you must understand what it will take to get you to level two, what is the process that is needed to get you to level two and the faculties needed to get there. At thinking level one, there are problems that you can only deal with at that level because at that level you are restricted in your abilities and understanding both mentally and spiritually. If you will solve, conquer, or address level two problems, you must be either at a higher thinking level or around the same level to understand level two problems to overcome them. I like to use the illustration of weight lifting because it is a gradual strength building sport. When a weight lifter is attempting to lift let us say 350 pounds, he does not lift that amount of weight immediately. He has tried and either failed to lift that amount of weight at some point. However with persistence and raw determination, he will eventually and gradually gain the strength and mental focus to lift that amount. He must have lifted 300lbs, 310lbs, or some other similar range before he can lift 350lbs.

The human body is incredible! The human mind extraordinary! Some linear significant physical and mental shift must occur before he can move to the next weight level. To go from one level to another requires a shift. It requires movement as I mentioned earlier. There can be no change without movement.

When I moved my family to Atlanta, Georgia, that was a geographic movement, process is the single most critical factor that precipitates change. I was walking through a mall in Atlanta recently and I was reflecting upon why some people are content to do the same jobs day after day and never seem to want a different type of life or existence. I discovered that therein lies the problem. Not many people desire to move to a different place in their life. Some people are just content with where they are. Some people's dreams limit them to a narrow and limited existence. I refer to this as the place of contentment. You must move to a place of discontentment with your life. There is more to life than what you actually see. Some people have never travelled out of their local city; travelling out of the United States is a stretch for them. Stretch yourself.

If you desire to lose weight for example, you must first make a mental and spiritual shift. Losing weight is not easy. There must be a firm shift within you to go from wanting to be comfortable with being the weight you are, to wanting to have a better body to height ratio. That desire has to be so strong that you are willing to move heaven and earth to achieve that goal. How badly you desire it will be evident in your ability to make the shift to discipline yourself to change your eating habits, cut calories, exercise more and do it consistently—all over again. You may also want to consider bariatric surgery or gastric bypass (if you are morbidly obese) please consult a dietitian. However, do something. Dr. John Maxwell in his book "The 21 Irrefutable Laws of Leadership,4" said it best… Decide Quickly, Take Action and Wait for the results.

If you want to see that change in your life, are you willing to sacrifice, (sacrifice is a multi-dimensional shift, an unselfish act) so that the changes can take place. Abraham in the Biblical Old Testament was willing to sacrifice his only son Isaac in obedience to God's requirement. He did not just give God lip service as some of us do. He saddled his mule the next day and began the journey (movement) to the mountain where God had instructed him to go. These are the kinds of sacrificial experiences that bring change, and promote significance. I have a son whom I love dearly (I have 2 kids), and I thought about the level of obedience and spiritual guts it takes to obey at that level and it just astounded me. You must be willing to go against the grain sometimes to accomplish great personal triumph. Nothing that is worthy or significant in accomplishing comes without great sacrifice.

This brings me to the next principle. You cannot go to the next level if you do not possess the correct set of knowledge. You cannot solve the big problems that have plagued you for years unless something exponentially bigger and newer has impacted your thinking, something that is more powerful and greater that is able to move the problem itself. That new information has to move you mentally, spiritually and philosophically. To demonstrate this principle let us look at water. If you have a glass of water that is half full and you place a piece of ice into that glass, you have inherently changed the volume of water that was originally there. By placing the ice into the glass, you have caused the amount of water to rise above its original level. THERE CANNOT BE CHANGE WITHOUT MOVEMENT.

When we struggle with life controlling problems, intrinsically we are at a momentary deficit. We do not always know who we are, what we are capable of, or what is it going to take to bring us out of that place of struggle. There is something dynamic and empowering about knowledge. Peter, the fisherman in the Biblical New Testament was asked by Jesus, " Who do men say that I am?" He answered unequivocally that Jesus was the Christ, the son of the living God. If you just give lip service to knowledge, it will show in your effectiveness, it will be evident in the results that ensure. However, if you really know Jesus it changes the equation in your life. You know him, he knows you. Peter knew who Jesus was, he spent countless hours with Him, he was there when Jesus was baptized, he also heard the great voice saying, "this is my beloved son in whom I am well pleased." 5 That knowledge was empowering to Peter and it can also be empowering to us. Know what you know and know what you do not know!

Let me further illustrate this principle: a computer is a powerful tool, but if you do not know how to use it, it remains a powerful tool that you do not know how to use. If you learn how to use it, then it becomes a powerful tool that you can now use to become more productive and add something new to your skill set. I am a great advocate of education because knowledge acquisition is really an investment in yourself. If you get a higher-level education simply to get a job, you are missing the point in knowledge acquisition. Getting an education is a navigation tool. If you have a problem that has stymied you from moving to a place of power in your life, perhaps you may do well to find out if there are any other individuals who have had similar problems and how they overcame. Make the journey of discovery; take the steps necessary to shift out of mediocrity into the glorious gnosis of who you are and who you can become. Read up on the subject, consult thought leaders, or find a mentor, find someone to walk with you, someone who has more information than you do to help you cross the spectrum of indifference and ignorance to greater knowledge empowerment.

I always believed that the more you know the more you can be. Essentially, you cannot rise above what you know. Your personal growth will be in the same proportion to which you acquire the relevant knowledge to understand the nature of the problem and yourself. It is not just knowledge that changes us but what I refer to as relevant displacement knowledge. I was discontented with my life several years ago and I decided to research my father. He left when I was three years old so I did not really know him. A couple of years ago, as I contemplated some of the generational weaknesses that I struggled with, I called my father's ex-wife (my then step-mother) and inquired if my father was married to her at the time when he fathered me with my mother and she said he was. This was new knowledge to me as it answered a lot of probing questions I had concerning my own struggles as a young man. It let me realize that the genetic disposition to be a philanderer was inside of me and was not by accident. They had a root.

Every problem has a root cause. Knowing that enabled me to break free of those bondages my father faced. Now I knew what I was facing, now I knew my real enemy. Now I knew what I had to do and the struggles seemed to be easier to face. Do your research, find out where you came from, what are some of the struggles with which your ancestors fought. If you are struggling with a life-debilitating problem, you may have to get desperate. Know for certain that left unchecked; it could be your ruin. Do something. Get creative. Pray! Reach higher than you have ever reached before. The problem with us sometimes is that we are either lazy and sometimes more fearful of the process than the resultant outcomes that our persistence can produce.

2

PURSUING SUSTAINABLE PERSONAL GROWTH:

HOW WE CONTINUE CHANGING
It is the capacity to develop and improve your skills that distinguishes leaders from followers.
BENNIS AND NANUS[6]

If you do not continue to grow and improve what I coined, "your personal effectiveness engine," you run the risk of personal obsolescence, irrelevance and spiritual dwarfism. There. I said it. The truth is we are not concerned with personal effectiveness, as we should because we have set no personal goals and personal targets we are trying to hit. We are content with being average. Mediocrity is addictive. Just ask Franky Schaffer[7]. In his book Addicted to Mediocrity … he says, "There are basically two reasons why an individual or a group makes a terrible mistake. One is outright stupidity and an inability to grasp the issue; the second is a false view of truth at some particular point— in other words the wrong foundation, the wrong principles, the wrong presuppositions."

I have always maintained that personal success is not an accident but a succession of carefully executed deliberate actions that meld strategically together to arrive at the desired end. I remember several years ago while driving through Decatur, Georgia on my way to work, I was having one of those philosophical conversations with God. I asked Him, What makes some people successful and others not? Why do some people get further ahead while others languish in a place of constant struggle? The answer came back, "Successful people do successful things." I kid you not. It may appear simplistic to you but there are some powerful and meaningful truths in that statement. Successful people have the capacity to change and grow in a way that separates them from others. I think of the Steve Jobs, the Rick Warrens, the Deepak Chopras and others who through diligence and discipline have been become leaders in their personal sphere of influence. The story is told about Larry Bird, who, every morning before he left for school would shoot 500 free throws. Success is not an accident!! He was undoubtedly one of the best in the NBA. The journey to that place of constant elevation was deliberate and inevitable. The discipline of constant elevation in one's life comes only through diligence and doing, revising and searching and refining the process all over again.

A friend of mine shared the story of Serena Young. Serena Young, he said is a classic example of RIS (risk inverse syndrome) and symbolic interactionism. Born in Taipei, Taiwan, in 1955, she was a quadriplegic, but after significant therapeutic strategies, life returned to her upper limbs but never returned to her lower limbs. Her parents moved from Taiwan to California, USA, where she spent 17 years not in junior high, college or university. She spent 17 years in a hospital, 1959-1976, moving on a wheelchair. One day the doctor expressed great sorrow. He told her that her life was wasted, that fate had been unkind to her, that she was destined to a life of abnormality. Her reply shocked the doctor. She told the doctor that one day she would replace him in spite of the fact that she was a late bloomer.

She explained that her time in the hospital was not wasted, that she was a diligent student over those years and studied several medical books. Additionally, her personal vision had shaped her tragedy and that no wheelchair would determine the size of her dreams. Do not let any wheelchair, any circumstance or inability, no disappointment, no tragedy, must determine the size of your dreams. Serena Young would never settle for silver and bronze when gold was available. Today she has in fact replaced that doctor.

What is your capacity for change? Are you growing? Are you in the same mental and spiritual condition you were three months ago, three years ago? As Bennis and Nanus[8] so rightfully posit that it is the capacity to develop and improve one's skills that invariably sets us apart. That capacity is the differentiator. It is that individual creative and personal reservoir that can be tapped, developed, or refilled constantly that will promote consistent change and growth. It is your courage capacity that enables you to go on even if the road ends. In order to continue to build your capacity, fill your reservoir, and improve your skills, new knowledge has to be introduced in the change process.

Whether it is a new skill or new experience, it is something that was not there before that brings the soul into a new place of change and growth.

Growth requires movement and movement promotes change. What you do not know in this instance can invariably hurt you. In order for you to move beyond your current state, you must introduce something new into the equation that was not there before to have a different experience. If you have not prayed like you should before, pray! If you have fallen out of love with your wife for example, become incapacitated by some life controlling habit, it means that something was introduced in the equation that was either toxic or unproductive. Or, as in the case of divorce, something was either removed from the equation, or has changed. Irrevocably, however, if you do nothing or add nothing to the equation, it gradually disintegrates or decomposes into a lifeless relationship. I have counseled many young men facing divorce or already divorced to discover that there was one common thread… somebody was growing and the other was not and a huge emotional, spiritual or even intellectual gap developed and caused them to gradually grow apart. *Sustainability is not an accident.*

The dynamics of the relationship between a man and a woman is not a static, abstract process that carries itself. It requires constant injection of new ideas and fuel to keep the flame alive. If you have lost the desire to love and care for that human being it becomes a game of pretense that ends in the divorce court. You cannot drive new dynamics in a relationship if you yourself do not *desire* to grow and change your condition. Human nature is very fickle, if you do not grow, you revert to a former lower state of ineffectiveness, and indifference sets in. My wife calls such individuals lazy lovers.

Just as plants and every living organism require external combined infusions of nutrients to grow, we as human beings require the "milk of new knowledge" to empower us to navigate unknown situational waters, difficult relationships, and business decisions. The more we know the better decision maker we become. Read more, spend time with those who know more than you, and seek to discover new opportunities to acquire knowledge that you did not have before. The process of acquiring new knowledge will in itself provide a learning experience and the knowledge acquired will take you to a completely new world of discovery.

PART TWO

THE ROLE OF MOVEMENT

3

THE NECESSITY OF MOVEMENT IN CHANGE AND GROWTH:
What Promotes Change
There can be no change without movement.
MARK GUEVARA

When Orville and Wilbur Wright made their first attempt at flight, they failed. Did that stop them from continuing to try? Absolutely not! The story is told about their early upbringing. Their father was a Methodist minister who exposed them to all kinds of scientific material on mathematics, physics, chemistry and other sources of learning. Hear me out here reader, they were exposed to sources of

There can be no change without movement.

knowledge that fed their creativity and innovative reservoir. They synthesized the knowledge they were exposed to into creative possibilities. The knowledge they gained and were exposed to, when synthesized into ideas, gave birth to possibilities. Their father sowed the seeds of creativity and flight possibilities by providing an environment of an open mind through the right kind of literature. This propelled their thinking to the possibility that even human flight was possible.

They were in the words of Robert Schuller, "Possibility Thinkers." As a young man, I remember reading an excerpt from Robert Schuller's book called Possibility Thinkers[9]. Shuller wrote that Possibility Thinkers fly an idea like a kite. They gradually give that idea buoyancy until it begins to gain momentum. That excerpt and the possibility thinking principle had a very profound effect on me as a young man, and has stayed with me to this day. The Wright Brothers did exactly that. Achieving flight was not something to be attained; they had flown in their creative minds and the idea of flight was thriving long before they actually begin that successful experiment. Useful knowledge drives ideas and it promotes personal growth. Take some time out of your busy schedule to gain some useful knowledge everyday. Make it a habit of reading a new book every month. Have a conversation with someone new. Go see an interesting movie or documentary. It is useful knowledge that promotes growth because it displaces ignorance. Ignorance presents barriers to change resolves. If you desire a closer relationship with God, the only way to achieve this is through a personal knowledge relationship with Him. Spend some more time to get to know him better. Peter in the Biblical New Testament cites "growing in grace in the knowledge of Jesus Christ." He also cites that as new born babes in Christ we must desire the sincere milk of the word that we may grow thereby."[10]

Knowledge is gained in many ways. It is taught and experienced; it is gained from sources of information such as books, magazines and from evaluated[11] experiences. The Wright Brothers experimented based on things they knew would possibly work. Possibility thinkers are risk takers. Do not be afraid to take risks. You may very well discover the next big thing. I have always maintained that if I had lost my job, it was all right. A job does not define who I am. The job is not the fuel that propels me. I know who I am, I know where I am going, and I know what I have. They may take the job but the knowledge within an individual is appositionally irreplaceable. Benjamin Franklin[12] once said "If a man empties his purse into his head, no one can take it from him. An investment in knowledge always pays the highest return." Maybe he knew something that many of us would be wise to apply.

As water goes from liquid to gaseous form, the process is movement. It is transformational movement or change of state. The catalyst is heat. Whatever level of growth you wish to accomplish will be determined by the quality and strength of the catalyst. The greater the catalyst the greater will be the proportionate growth. Many individuals do not attain growth because for some strange reason they do not see or visualize themselves as becoming a new individual or having a new dynamic in their life. You cannot be comfortable with your life and expect to experience change and growth. You have to be willing to leave the familiar and mundanely comfortable and venture in new and unknown territories in your life. By venturing into new territory you will experience what Dr. John Maxwell[13] refers to as a period of discovery. Do not be afraid of the catalyst, good change is good.

I had a conversation with my son and I was asking him about his own ability to score well in an upcoming SAT test he was about to take. For some strange reason, he could not at first see himself as capable of scoring high. He was comparing himself with some of his peers and their past performance on the test. He limited himself by what he knew! I took this opportunity to give him new information about himself by relating some of his own experiences and accomplishments. I had to provide him with a new frame of reference. I also told him that in order to be able to perform at a higher level, he had to make some changes in his thinking. I used the metaphor of a tree. He did get it and scored well beyond what he was expecting.

> *I believe that as fruit bearing is a sign of growth and maturity, so the type of fruit you produce is an indication of your function, purpose and destiny.*

I believe that as fruit bearing is a sign of growth and maturity, so, the type of fruit you produce is an indication of your character, ability, and purpose. The ability to think creatively requires a special kind of individual. Wilber and Orville Wright were special. You and I can soar; we can create things and design business ideas that can change the lives of people and the world. Look at Steve Jobs and what he did at Apple Computer. We must however, be willing to endure the mortar and pestle in the crucible of patience and creativity. Every living tree under heaven has a specific character, specific ability and specific purpose. That is how God created them. Mango trees have within themselves, within their biological DNA, an inherent ability to produce mangoes. Apple trees have the same ability. If you want to produce a different kind of fruit which change calls for, you must become a different kind of tree. You have to change.

4

THE FLIGHT METAPHOR:
RELATING FLIGHT TO THE GROWTH PROCESS

Flight and growth are both multi-dimensional. Just as flight is not simply upward elevation, so personal growth is not just intellectual ascent.
MARK GUEVARA

The Wright brothers conceived their dream of flying in Dayton, Ohio. They could not however, manifest or materialize their dream in Dayton. They discovered that the winds were not favorable for flying. They simply had to move. As you remember in an earlier chapter, *there can be no change without movement.* They had learned after researching and making some pertinent phone calls, that the right environment and favorable winds were available to literally fly their theory in the Cape Hatteras section of the Carolinas coast. That theory was that strong sustainable winds were needed to buoy the flight of a man in a sophisticated kite.

We can safely deduct that it is not only good but also sometimes necessary to move for your life to take flight. Orville and Wilbur had done all they could possibly do within their current environment and resources to get off the ground in Dayton, Ohio. They had conceived the possibility of flying and the right elements necessary to test their theory, now they needed the right environment to fly their idea (to borrow a phrase from Dr. Robert Shuller's book, Possibility Thinkers). It is obvious from what we have discovered so far that the Wright brothers were possibility thinkers.

In order for you as an individual to move from a place of failure and stagnation to a place of high effectiveness, the dynamics that create and promote high flight and constant upward movement must be at work. Consider a car. As fast as they have been able to make them, they still cannot fly. Insanely record land speeds have been chronicled about man's ingenuity with highly modified cars. For a car to fly, it has to be either transformed into a Helicar,[14] or retrofitted with the right kind of propellers and engines to enable flight. If you have tried to take flight and move beyond your present level of effectiveness, you either need retrofitting with wings of knowledge or major transformation. There simply is no other way. Flight is only possible under the right conditions.

What if the conditions are not favorable? What are favorable conditions? These are both great questions and only you may be able to answer them. We all make decisions from different reservoirs of information. I will share my experiences with you however and what I did. In 1996, my wife and I were contemplating moving from New York City. Our two kids were climbing the wall of our small two-bedroom apartment. I did two things when making the decision as to where to move. I researched and prayed. I then asked myself these questions:

Will I have a good support system?

Will it sustain or improve my quality of life?

(This was specific to me) Did it have a good business environment for entrepreneurs?

Your questions will be different but only you

and God can answer them. We settled on Atlanta, Georgia. Money Magazine at the time (who I worked for), said that Atlanta was third on the list for best cities for entrepreneurs. The other cities were Seattle, Washington and Portland, Oregon. Not likely cities for me at the time considering the weather patterns. It was also a good move for us as a family as my brother had recently moved to Atlanta. One of my best friends had been living here for quite some time already so the support system was there. Also, during a Christmas visit we noticed that the kids were running outside in the winter and this appealed to us. It turned out to be a great move for us. We prospered in Atlanta in many ways.

Bad habits sometimes need a vacation. If you have been struggling with life controlling and goal debilitating habits such as sexual addiction, pornography, overeating (to a lesser extend as this may require professional help), lack of discipline to exercise, moving to a different location may enable you to shift focus and the change in environment may facilitate a change in habit. When on a vacation, use that time to not only rest and relax but to refocus and make an intentional effort to shed bad habits. Being away from the familiar environment briefly may encourage habit change and new habit formations.

I recently reconnected with a dear friend who I had not seen in about 3 years. She had bariatric surgery to lose weight. Her transformation was astounding! She demonstrated to me how desperate she had become and how deep her well of desire was to bring her weight down to a period in her life 20 years before. Prior to her divorce, she was just miserable. Her husband ignored her so she found solace in writing, food, Solitaire, television, and Netflix[15]. She was so miserable that she had eaten her way up to 300 pounds. Relishing her newfound freedom, she decided to reinvent herself. She moved to another state, (sometimes geographical movement is necessary to achieve your growth objectives) and decided after consulting with her doctor to have gastric bypass surgery. She looked fabulous and was happy with her newfound fat-free person. Was this drastic? Yes it was. Was it necessary? Yes, for her it was. You will have to ask yourself how far am I willing to go, to move beyond where I am, to get to where I really want to be.

5

EAGLE OR JET? HOW HIGH DO YOU WANT TO FLY?

RELATING FLIGHT TO DESIRE
The heights by great men reached and kept, were not obtained by sudden flight, But they, while their companions slept, were toiling upward in the night.
HENRY WADSWORTH LONGFELLOW.

Just as desire must precede change, intensity must precede height or depth of change. You must develop an unsinkable attitude and unwavering focus for constant elevation and high performance. As I was writing this chapter, one of my closest friends was lying in the intensive care unit of a hospital in Burlington, Massachusetts. He had left his family in Atlanta, Georgia to work in Boston because he could not find work in the Atlanta metro area. We had spoken on several occasions about the way things were shaping up in the economy and how at times we have to make the tough decisions to gain momentum and change the dynamics of living. The reason I am sharing this story is to illustrate the value of indefatigable persistence, many people let go and give up when faced with disastrous and life changing circumstances. He never gave up, he never made excuses and we shared a common mantra "For God's sake don't give up."

Invariably every one of us fights and deals with life's challenges from different perspectives but it is this perspective, this distinct view or image of our capabilities and resources, that enables us to quickly overcome or go under. This chapter deals with movement.

I used to liken personal growth to that of an eagle. I have however since changed that allegory. I changed it because further research caused me to overhaul my thinking. An eagle we all know can fly at very high altitudes, sometimes as high as 15000 feet. However, as high as an eagle can fly it has limitations as to how high it can fly, how fast it can fly and what load it can carry at those altitudes. Inherent within the eagle is its limited physical ability. My point—you can continue to fly like an eagle but you can only soar so high and fly so fast and your payload is limited.

An airplane however, is a different matter altogether. Although the airplane got its initial flying lessons from birds, the similarity ends quickly. An airplane can climb to heights upwards of 35000 feet and in some cases higher. While an unfair comparison, the objective is to draw our attention to quantity of capability and greater capacity for higher payloads and velocities. An eagle can only carry its young during flight. An airplane however, can carry several hundred people, an accomplishment that is mind-boggling with its size and at those heights. An eagle can fly fast but an airplane can fly faster and possibly stay longer in the air as long as there is enough fuel. I found myself desiring to be like an airplane. I can carry more people with me. Good leaders desire to transform and influence as many lives as they possibly can. A leader is only as great as his ability to influence and carry others along with him. No good leader is good by himself. As an eagle I am limited in my capability to fly very high and very far. As an airplane, my capabilities for flight and movement are much more favorable. My capacity is greater and my navigational capabilities are now more advanced. I can now go to new places and quickly get back to base. Airplanes can be equipped with sophisticated technology to do reconnaissance missions, to even refuel other airplanes, carry extremely large amounts of cargo and fly at extremely high altitudes and extremely long distances without stopping for fuel. We must not limit ourselves by our perspective. Change your perspective and whole new worlds of possibilities are now available to you. When you shift your perspective, when you change your mind set and of course when you change your thinking, the scenery changes. It is said that if you are not the lead dog, the scenery never changes. Become a lead dog, shift your mind from being an eagle to that of an airplane and the possibilities of a different life become not a dream but a real manifestation.

Many of us actually live and perform in life well below our real capabilities. You should be flying like an airplane instead of an ordinary eagle. Larry Bird, the great basketball player of the Boston Celtics proved to the world that discipline and stellar work ethic could change your destiny. It is reported that Larry Bird would practice constantly and every day… shooting in the dark. He reportedly said that poverty drove him to be best at what he did. If your life is not going the way you like. You can change it. I did. I left a foreign country to attend college. I barely had enough money, in New York City as a total stranger, but an intense desire to study and change the trajectory of my life. I finished my entire course work almost a year ahead of schedule while holding down a college job.

    I know a man who is the one of the most talented individuals I have ever met. He plays the guitar like a virtuoso; he paints like Renoir and composes effortlessly. But like many other great men he had a problem with his personal sexual discipline and has made a royal mess of his life and the lives of the children he has sired. He is not unlike many young men who have taken to decision making by their emotions. Obviously talent is not enough. The Tiger Woods, the Kobe Bryants, and many others who had airplane capability but succumbed to low-flying desires are enough examples for us to take note and heed. We were however, designed to make better decisions by our will, our emotions and our intellect. Desire to become a faster, stronger performer than you currently are. It is the beginning of great things for you.

6

HOW HIGH CAN YOU FLY?
The role of your Desire

Your personal drive and efficiency as a human being is intricately interwoven in your own ability to do and be.
FRANCES HESSELBEIN

I am eternally grateful to my wife for introducing me to books filled with principles that have helped move me to a place of higher thinking. It was through those seminal moments that my love for philosophy grew exponentially. Now I have become a serious student of personal growth philosophy and I hope to share with you in these brief chapters not only strong change and growth philosophies but how they have also impacted my own life as well and have taken me to a whole different place in my life. I have read books by some of the great thought leaders of our time who by virtue of things they experienced, mentally crucibled powerful and profound life-changing principles.

As we referred earlier on in the foreword to Stedman Graham's interview with Larry King, when he said that every one of us has twenty-four hours in a day at our disposal, let us look at that statement as it relates to our intent. Frances Hesselbein in her book <u>Leader of the Future</u>[16], made a profound statement that reverberates with me to this day. It is simply irrefutable. She said that one's personal drive and efficiency, as a human being is intricately interwoven in their own ability to do and be. Invariably, you cannot rise above your own weaknesses if you are not able to rise above who you are, if you are not able to constantly shift and change. Many of us wish to acquire wealth and to be more effective but we simply are not *able* and *willing* to put the time and effort that is required to get there. We sit on the sidelines and are spectators while others are doing what we can do if we get up from our bad perspectives. My friend, I have lived long enough to understand that life is not a spectator sport. The people who are enjoying life and reaping the rewards are those who are doing and becoming.

This chapter is about destination.

After listening to Stedman Graham on that fateful day, something happened to me. What happened to me must happen to you if you want to change. I did not read his book back then but what he said was enough to get me started. I wanted to maximize my time because what he said was simply true. How we use our time is a direct reflection of our own ability to effect change and build synergy in our own lives. I was deeply moved by what he said. I was moved to the point where I left the room where our family was and went to lie down on my son's bunk bed to think about what he said and how I could maximize my 24 hours. (Stedman, thank you). I soon drifted asleep.

When I awoke the next morning, (no one awoke me from my son's bed). I awoke with this great idea of dividing my day into four six-hour periods. I had not read this anywhere although I am sure that there are books written about time management in this way. However, this was my own *revelation*. It came from my own reservoir. I am not a morning person but I decided to change my habits to accommodate the maximizing of my twenty-four hours. I became a morning person. Here is what I did.

1 The first six hours, which is from 6:00 am to 12: 00 noon, I decided to dedicate to the critical things that have the most potential to wreck my day, or as Stephen Covey puts it, the boulders. I am up either before or by 6 am. I review the day's activities and prioritize. It is critical to prioritize. If you do not prioritize, you run the risk of allowing other events to distract and take you off course. There are simply way too many distractions in a regular day. How do you prioritize? Do the things that are most important to your life or work. You must have a value system that directs your thinking and governs your life. My family comes first, my health and then anything that has the potential for the most revenue generating opportunity comes after. Get your exercise in before the day begins. I generally got my kids to school first then I run for about 30 to 45 minutes. I run daily. Research has shown that the earlier we exercise the better our bodies' metabolism responds; we feel more energized and increase sharpness in our thinking.

Eat a healthy breakfast. A healthy breakfast by the way is not donuts and coffee. It is not Starbucks coffee and a scone or Danish either. Consult a qualified dietitian (I consulted mine) for tips and ideas for what constitutes a healthy breakfast and perhaps you may even consider changing your eating habits. The point here is your health is your greatest personal asset. If you are a business leader, consider what has the most potential to either drive your profits, make Wall Street happy, or destroy your competitive lead and drive shareholder value way up. If reading the newspaper is important to you, consider getting a summary of the days news either in electronic format or via email. You may also consider subscribing to Soundview,[17] an online resource for book summaries that can be downloaded in mp3, Adobe Acrobat PDF or other audio formats to your Apple iPod or your Amazon Kindle. It takes less time to read and you would have gotten the information that you need. Instead, focus on the upcoming events and rehearse your plan and mode of attack.

If a round of golf with an important client is critical, do so. As you develop your own set of values and priorities, your first six hours will change. It is not only what is important, but also what is critical. Place a high or low scale on your list of to dos. Try not to over schedule.

Target a few things to get done. You only have sixteen hours of useful productive hours. Just ensure that it is all prioritized and value based. Also make use of a scheduling device either a datebook or an electronic datebook that enables you to track your time. If you cannot track your time, you will not be able to measure your effectiveness. If you are home please avoid watching TV, it robs you of meaningful productive creative moments in your life. This worked for me.

2

The second six hours, which is generally from 12:00 noon to 6:00 p.m., I decided to devote to the non-critical issues. Let me emphatically say that this is only a suggestion and not a hard and fast set of carved out time management rules that you have to adhere to religiously. The objective here is to use your time wisely by prioritizing and maximizing your twenty-four hours. If this is important to you then time becomes precious. Non-critical issues will again vary on priorities and values. It is clearly important to ensure that you set your own Value Compass.[18] It is also important to schedule things that if not checked could throw off your schedule. Things like meeting with someone who has a tendency to talk too much.

I am serious. As a side note, please take some time to examine your relationships and determine if they are hurting or helping to build your value system. Some relationships we can all attest are toxic because they steal your time and the relationships are based on what you have and not who you are. Take a serious look at them. Some may have to go away. You decide.

The third 6-hour period is from 6:00 p.m. to 12:00 midnight. This is the time quadrant where, for some, non-business activities can be enjoyed or conducted. By the way, the weight of importance can be adjusted or moved around to suit your own personal lifestyle. If you are a night owl or work non-standard shift hours, reorganize the time to suit your set of values and priorities. This is the time where you set aside time for family, recreation, relaxation, and personal growth and unwind time.

I did not stop there. I have continued to change my entire habits as a human being. I now run every day. I always ran but not everyday and not consistently. This is something I decided to do to improve my odds of living a healthier life and taking serious considerations of genetic dispositions. Will it impact my health? Sure it will. I am doing something the generation that impacted my genetics did not do. I am adding something to the equation of healthy living that was not there before.

It would be unfair to speak of time and not leave the reader with some warnings about the dangers and pitfalls that accompany a character that is prone to tardiness. Let us begin by identifying tardiness for what it is. *Tardiness is the habitual inability to be in place on a scheduled time where the expected events occur after you have arrived.* Let me continue by saying that tardiness is a very bad habit that is correctable! However, chronic tardiness can cost you a future job, a business opportunity, or a date with a beautiful woman or man. In many instances you can miss a beautiful sunset, the birth of a child, or another opportunity that may never come again. When you are late, you have run out of time for the immediate opportunity. I lost my very first job due to tardiness. That was the last time that happened to me however.

Being tardy does not necessary mean that you are slow. If you move slowly due to a physical impairment, however, this does not necessarily contribute to your tardiness. Research shows that the real roots of tardiness are multifaceted. Poverty, poor mental organization, your time perspective and planning contribute to tardiness as well. However, there are real environmental factors that impact these roots. If Johnny is never taught about the importance of respecting the time of others, he may develop a tardy personality. Again, if at a home there are poor conditions that prevent Jenny from taking a shower or getting a solid breakfast before heading to school, this will prevent her from consistently being on time at school for example. In my case, no one told me about the importance of being on time as a child so it was not in my organizational vocabulary. It was not important to me. Additionally, I had to go to a river in the dark in the back of the house to take a bath before heading to school and to my first job. Those who are arrogant and think that being on time does not apply to them, must know that life is full of deadlines. Time management is extremely important because every opportunity has an expiration date. Never forget that! These tips will help you develop new habits to beat the tardiness bug

I. Get a working watch and set specific time

alarms.
II. Go to bed early if you can.
III. Set priorities… do what is important first
IV. Use a planner to keep track of the day's important activities
V. When you have an appointment, leave so that you have half an hour to 15 minutes to spare when you arrive. This will help you avoid last minute accidents.
VI. Call ahead for directions so you know where you are going. If you have access to the Internet, Googlemap or MapQuest the directions.
VII. If you have an appointment tomorrow, prepare what you will wear the day before.
VIII. Avoid last minute things to do.
IX. Watch your time so you can stay focused on time deadlines.
X. Stay focused.

PART THREE

FOCUS ON DESTINATION

7

THE ROLE OF KNOWLEDGE IN PERSONAL GROWTH

How knowledge makes you a better decision maker

If you know the enemy and know yourself, you need not fear the results of a hundred battles.
SUN TZU

I believe that if I know where I am going, I will get there quicker than if I did not have the way to get there. Having useful knowledge is part of the plan. What am I saying? Sun Tzu in his book *The Art of War* said something rather profound; *if you know the enemy and know yourself, you need not fear the result of a hundred battles.*[19] Although a bit epistemological, the role of knowledge cannot be down played nor minimized in its importance and strategic role in our effectiveness. The majority of people, who have been successful individuals, have one thing in common—navigable knowledge. Navigable Knowledge™ for the sake of this writing is knowledge that you can use or synthesize to get through difficult situations, make better decisions in times of crisis or navigate your way out of unfamiliar territory. It enables you to make critical life-changing decisions and take the necessary action as well. It is knowledge that has to be combined with common sense and risk. It is knowledge that is malleable and the underlying principles that they contain can be redesigned, re-engineered, refocused or varied to work in diverse situations regardless of the operating environment and the prevailing circumstances.

If you are going to start a new business, design a new product, or begin a new journey, you must have an idea of the operating environment you will be facing. How do companies or individuals navigate unfamiliar market environments and succeed? If you do not know and are unwilling to take risk, you are at a great disadvantage. The outcome of some risks is calculable and some are to a certain extent predictable. Invariably, however, the individual with sufficient knowledge, chutzpah and fearlessness will succeed faster than the one without these elements and thereby reduce his risk.

Risk is really a game of chance. Some of our troops roll the dice every day with each step they take in mine-infested territory. As I began to write this book, I discovered that this book came about as I thought about my son Seth and daughter Ysatis and how carefully and deliberately exposing them to risk has prepared them to take risks in some measure. Ysatis is fearless, enterprising, entrepreneurial and not afraid of bungee jumping, and monster roller coaster rides that will scare the bravest of mortals. Seth on the other hand, is a careful analytical and calculated risk taker.

Risk is a bad word in some circles. In others it is necessary. In financial investment transactions, unfortunately the greater the rewards mantra does not always work. There are countless investors who have lost just about everything. In an extremely volatile market risk becomes a calculating science. In determining and navigating a difficult surgery, risk in the form of a risky procedure, may be the only option to save a life. In deciding to crash in a populated area or on water, landing on water may be the better risk option. Just ask Captain Sullenberger of the US Airways flight 1549 he had to land on the Hudson River in New York City. Getting married these days is a major crapshoot. The divorce rate continues to climb.

While I certainly understand that we take risks everyday, many may not be aware of the level of risk. It is certainly a statistical numbers game for the insurance companies. Risk is measured by where you live, the lifestyle you lead, the car and length of distance you drive, whether you are a frequent skydiver or play it safe. A life of risk can be short lived and exciting or it can be long, rewarding and meaningful.

We may be familiar with the importance or benefits of reading but somewhere I think we have placed the primacy and value on reading and not enough emphasis on the benefits of knowledge acquisition. I recently read an article online where Steve Jobs, (the CEO of Apple Computer's), opined rather negatively on the new digital reader from Amazon called the kindle. I quote *"It doesn't matter how good or bad the product is, the fact is that people don't read anymore,"* he said. *"Forty percent of the people in the*

U.S. read one book or less last year. The whole conception is flawed at the top because people don't read anymore." Steve Jobs must know something we do not know. The approach that Apple has taken to marketing and selling their digital lifestyle products is legendary. Oprah is also using the Kindle. Although reading is the most common vehicle or leading activity to acquire knowledge, it is not the only vehicle. Knowledge can be gleaned from visual mediums such as videos, (the preferred medium of the YouTube™ generation), audio books, experiential events, one-on-one sessions, attending speaking conferences and experimentation.

In our new knowledge economy, the Internet has risen to become not only the dominant marketing tool, but also the biggest repository of knowledge resources. Wikis and websites are everywhere. Recent studies[20] have shown that Internet usage has proven to be invaluable to individuals through the promulgation and creation of information resources. This will indeed change the marketing landscape for companies as they promote products and services to knowledge focused consumers. Many consumers research products and companies on the Internet before purchasing. Indeed before I purchase anything new whether they are electronics, cars or even large-scale investments such as mortgages and similar purchases, I always check the Internet to see if there are other options available to me and perhaps get a sneak peek under the hood before I commit money.

Many mistakes and pitfalls could have been avoided if more thorough research had been done prior to execution or launch. There is a very fine line between risk and insanity. Successful businesses can only go as far as their knowledge of customers' needs and market conditions can take them. You and I will only become more resourceful, competent, and better decision makers when we have the requisite knowledge to take action and effectively execute successful plans. T-Boone Pickens, whom I admire immensely, said that his father told him " A fool with a plan can outsmart a genius with no plan any day of the week."

8

IMPEDIMENTS TO FLIGHT:
DEALING WITH OBSTACLES
Obstacles are opportunities to solve problems...
MARC GUEVARA

I cannot emphasize enough, the importance of knowing. Sun Tzu said that anyone going to war in a new territory must be familiar with the surrounding territory and landscape to gain a competitive advantage against the enemy. Someone may ask, what if I do not know? Well, you may not know everything but you will have some knowledge with which you can proceed. I will be the first to admit that I am a huge risk-taker, however, the more knowledge I have of the territorial demographics and prevailing conditions market or otherwise, the better the possibility of success.

One may also ask with the uncertainty of the

current market with falling retail giants, failing banks, dwindling savings and disappearing 401KS, what do I do. Is it safe to wait? I recently sat with a friend of mine who was wiped out of a significant portion of her retirement. Her story broke my heart. She trusted two investment bankers with her savings and they both lost significant portions of her savings. Be careful to whom you entrust your money. Get a first, second and third opinion. It never hurts. She also said that she had this gut feeling that something was going to go wrong. It did. Nothing is wrong in asking reliable friends to provide alternative sources to ensure that you are making decisions based on trusted sources of knowledge. There is a lot of information out there, not a whole lot of usable knowledge.

Who is your enemy? My definition: anything, person, a weakness, places, or pending event about which or whom you know very little or are totally unfamiliar. Essentially, what you do not know can eventually hurt you. The following are some of the reasons why dreams do not get fulfilled and become flights of fancy instead.

 **WE WAIT TOO LONG AND WASTE PRECIOUS TIME BEFORE WE EXECUTE A PLAN OR TAKE ADVANTAGE OF AN OPPORTUNITY.**

I sincerely believe that every opportunity or noble undertaking has to take place or be accomplished within a given space of time. Every opportunity has an expiration date. Why is it that we cannot plant corn every month of the year or flowers bloom at a certain time of the year? My point is this: *There is no time like now.* While the idea is fresh in your mind, while you desire to do something great, while you desire to accomplish something you have never done. Do it now! The time to execute is now. I profoundly believe what Dr. John Maxwell said in his book *The 21 Irrefutable Laws of Leadership,* Decide Quickly, Take Action and Wait for the results. Got something unique? Put it out there as quickly as possible and wait for the results.

 # WE MAKE EXCUSES INSTEAD OF USING OUR GOD GIVEN CREATIVITY

A couple years ago, I met this great leader named Paul Boudreau. Paul was a great mentor and friend. He always had slithers of wisdom to share with me and they have stayed with me to this day. One of those was " You cannot make excuses and money at the same time." It may not have been his original thinking but he was the one who shared it with me. We all at some time have found ourselves in difficult situations that we thought that we would never escape. However, those of us creative ones, in desperation tried everything until something worked. I know first hand what I am sharing with you here. Having escaped the clutches of poverty, I can only say that having little has taught me to use my imagination in ways others would normally not do. We make excuses because we lack creativity. My father left when I was 3 years old. I struggled as a young man in areas where a young man needs his father for guidance. It was easy for me to blame my life's misfortunes on not having a father, but I discovered that I either get busy living or make excuses for the rest of my life. I discovered reading early, and I found an old book on etiquette that served to provide invaluable knowledge on being a more chivalry-minded gentleman than others my age. Excuses are for those who are mentally lazy. Adverse situations are really opportunities to solve problems. In business, the more problems you solve, the more valuable you become to your organization. Use your imagination to get creative and solve problems and get out of situations that could possibly kill or harm you.

3. WE SET UNREALISTIC GOALS THAT ARE OUTSIDE OUR GIFTING.

A couple years ago, I was very privileged to sit at the feet of Peter Daniels and listen to him as he spoke about some of the events and principles that shaped his life and successes. One of those he said was " If you are going into any business undertaking, make sure that you have the requisite skills and knowledge to see it from start to finish." A business plan is good but business savvy is better. Knowing your market is good but having a product or service to match that market is better. Do an assessment. Analyze all of your assets to undertake any task. Do your homework, study before any undertaking, and be absolutely sure that you have what it takes to see your plan from concept to execution. Go for sustainability not fluff. If you do not have the requisite skills, engage the help of trusted allies who have the missing elements of your endeavor or project.

WE SIMPLY SET NO GOALS AT ALL OR FAIL TO PREPARE

All goals seek to do is provide a frame of reference for the direction we want to take. Goals and plans are the mechanisms to give buoyancy to effective leadership. I remember gleaning some wisdom from a gentleman with whom I once worked. He was sharp, intelligent and focused. He told me as a young manager at Esteé Lauder, always have an objective in mind when you approach any task. Steve Tieman, thank you. These may seem as simplistic but many people just dive headfirst into a project or task and fail headfirst. The science and practice of project and program management has taken on a whole new meaning in the new knowledge economy. A project if it is going to be successful requires a starting point, a terminating point and the resources to ensure its successful completion. By the way, if you are going to entrust anyone with a project or major task, make sure that you give him or her everything they need to succeed. That is good leadership.

Many young people are floundering in high school and college simply because they have not set their sights higher nor have a specific goal or dream to which they aspire. *Specificity puts a deliberate marker on something you hope to achieve.* A specific goal is key. Consequently, improper planning or mental mapping is like embarking upon a journey and expecting to get there without the correct address. It simply would not work. The world is filled with well-meaning gifted individuals who think that natural gifts alone will get them to their desired success objectives. It is wise to also specialize in a specific area of interest or passion.

WE DO NOT BUILD RELATIONSHIPS WITH THOSE WHO CAN HELP

No man or woman is an island. At any given point in his or her life a person does not always have all the knowledge or skills that he/she needs to accomplish their goals. *Those of us with big dreams simply cannot accomplish those ideas without the help of others.* That being said, choose your allies and business relationships like you choose those important things in your life. Not everyone is helpful. Be wise enough to ascertain and discern those individuals who can drive your ideas further. Some relationships are toxic. Know when it is time to move away from those kinds of relationships. There are many kind and willing individuals but that does not necessarily mean that they have the wisdom and knowledge that you need to take your ideas successfully into the future.

6

SOME ARE AFRAID TO TAKE RISKS

Risk and reward are inseparable companions. It is true that if one takes a great risk, the reward is even greater. Although all risk has varying consequences, associated cost and uncertain outcomes, not taking risks or inaction many times has even more severe consequential outcomes. You must have a certain amount of chutzpah and raw determination to be a good risk-taker. The culture of fraud and bad risk has left some afraid to take anymore risk. However, a true risk-taker is sometimes knowledgeable in his area of enterprise and has made mistakes through trial and error. Some parents are justifiably afraid to let their kids overnight at their kids' friends' homes due to stuff they may have read or are simply afraid that something will happen to their kids. This is a different world we live in. One way to raise well-rounded kids who must stand on their own and take their own calculated risks is to expose them to as many sources of learning like movies, concerts, visiting other churches, museums, and family-trips. These are learning experiences that promote individual thinking and drive creativity. You expose them to a world that they may not have known exist or things they may have thought were not possible. My kids have many friends from all walks of like. My wife and I chose to expose them so they will have a wholesome expansive view of the world. And yes, check out your kids' friends and get to know their parents so you may know with whom you can let them overnight.

WHAT IS A RISK-TAKER? ARE RISKS ALWAYS NECESSARY?

A risk-taker as defined by this author is simply the following: any individual who is statistically crazy enough to take on a statistically dangerous task with a statistically unknown outcome. You have to be crazy to believe that it is possible to fly a kite large enough to hold a man and it will remain long enough in the air. You have to be crazy to believe that you will survive a fall from one of the tallest waterfalls in a kayak. But men have done just that. The Wright brothers believed that flight by man was possible even though at that time it was statistically impossible. Tyler Bradt survived an 18-story descent from the state of Washington's Palouse Falls in a kayak to set a record and make history at the same time. When asked why he did it…he said he just thought that is was possible. Barack Obama took a risk when he ran for the presidency in 2008. No short-term senator had ever taken such a risk and succeeded.

Buying a lottery ticket does not make you a risk-taker; you are simply a fool. Driving drunk or sleeping with people you do not know is not only patently stupid it is also statistically risky and you may be signing your death warrant. Obviously, common sense is not as common as we think.

8 WE ARE SIMPLY FEARFUL OF FAILURE

Fear is a paralyzing emotion. Good leaders, successful entrepreneurs and rich risk-takers have one thing in common… they are fearless. That being said, some people are still afraid to take any kind of risk. There are individuals who have great ideas but are afraid to risk money on ideas that could earn them fortunes. Understandably, if you have failed before, the chance taking becomes an anathema. But failure in certain enterprises should not produce sustainable fear of success. If you have failed in the past, do a reassessment of your past failure and trace the steps and resources used, analyze the feasibility of your plans and ideas, get an expert in your area of enterprise, or partner with someone who has way more experience than you. Because there simply is no reason to become fearful because of past failure. Take action, do something different that you did not do before, get creative and watch your fears disappear.

9. WE HAVE WEAKNESSES THAT DIMINISH OUR ABILITIES AND DILUTE OUR CHARACTER.

I will be painfully honest with you reader, personal character weaknesses do diminish our abilities and promote a person of sub-par character. Recently the governor of South Carolina Mark Sanford admitted an illicit affair with a woman.

He deliberately left out key details of his tryst as he spoke to the media. He then revealed that this was a pattern of behavior and had been a problem for him; it was an area of weakness. These instances along with countless other episodes of what I refer to as "character assassinations" are substantial and provoking evidence, that sexual weaknesses, lying, and stealing, diminish our ability to lead, to be reliable, to be credible, and to be a man or woman of integrity. If left unchecked they make the destination unreachable. One invariably becomes the kind of person or develops character that is questionable by the **footprints of weakness and bad decision-making you leave behind.** A tree is known by the kinds of fruit it produces. I had an apple tree in my backyard. Every fruit-bearing season it disappointed me. It produced bad apples every season without fail because something was inherently wrong with its ability to produce good apples consistently. Simply consider changing so you can begin to produce a life that is fruitful and deliver results that are indicative of a great individual.

> *Every opportunity has an expiration date.*

WE GIVE UP TOO EASILY WHEN OBSTACLES COME

I will be the first to admit that at first I really did not understand what obstacles really were. But as I grew and confronted barriers in education, business and other areas of my life, I began to get a first hand intimate knowledge. Obstacles from my perspective are seemingly impossible mental, physical, spiritual and emotional roadblocks. Sure there are business obstacles they could be environmental, regulatory, financial and otherwise. They seem to stand in your way of achieving great things. But I firmly believe that obstacles are real opportunities to solve problems. I remember reading a story about a man who had purchased some gold mining equipment during the gold rush in Southeastern Pennsylvania. This was before the gold rush in the West. He began mining and had marginal success finding small gold deposits. After a relatively short time, he gave up and sold the mining equipment to a real hungry prospector. It is said that, sixteen feet from where the previous prospector stopped, the largest gold deposits were found! This is a classic case of perseverance. In our 'instant" everything culture, it is hard to find those who will persevere until they get the desired results. If the results do not come in the first try some people simply give up. The Book of Proverbs chapter 24 verse 10 says, "if you faint in the day of adversity, your strength is small." In 1981 I went to the American embassy to obtain a student visa to study music at a New York music conservatory. The first time I went to apply for it was on a Monday, I was denied. I was disappointed but not discouraged. I had, from early on, as a young man having experienced the power of perseverance and prayer in difficult moments in my life and was not deterred. I always thought like a problem solver. This was in the space of three days. I had already quit my job, I had my plane ticket and people thought I was crazy. I needed some additional documents that normally took months to complete. I implored the bank to prepare the needed documents. They completed the documents in one day! I returned on Wednesday got my visa. I always believed that obstacles were opportunities to solve problems. Think like a problem solver at every turn.

WE DO NOT ALWAYS RISE WHEN WE FALL DOWN

I have the utmost admiration for those rare companies and individuals who rise triumphantly after a devastating and life-threatening event. Apple Computer for whose products I have a computing and user preference, made an amazing comeback in 1997 under Steve Jobs. They almost went belly-up in 1995. It is okay to make mistakes in the early years of learning and innovation. However, when stiff competition comes that mind set needs to change. Many of us have failed and made many mistakes. Those of us who rise do so by virtue of a choice to keep fighting. Those who do not rise do not rise for the same reason. How you fall (for not wanting to sound clichéd), is irrelevant. It is how and when you rise that sets the tone for the rest of your life.

This is not about those who have struggled initially and then became wealthy. Those are rags to riches story and I admire them wholeheartedly. This is about those who fall hard. They fall in sin publicly and privately, politicians, presidents, corporate CEOs alike and simple people who go down hard! We all have an inner compass that drives and guides us, whether it is a spiritual or moral compass, we act and make decisions from that reservoir. You make a mistake once, I call that an accident. Perhaps you were not having such a good day or you did not get enough sleep. But if you repeat that mistake over a number of years consistently, you have a problem that needs to be addressed. In my own life, I have struggled with mistakes that I constantly made. I never took the time to address them until my son was born. Those of you who are struggling with sexual issues, I have something that I want to share with you. This changed my life. When my desire for sex is high as it often is, I discovered that those were some of my most creative moments. We were made in God's image and likeness. No one can deny, that part of that likeness was the ability to create, to reproduce, to use the imagination in unique ways. Once I made that discovery, many things changed in my life. That was a pivotal revelation for me. When you are in the sexual zone, take some time to focus on the bigger reason you are here.

WE LACK FOCUS

Focus I discovered personally is the fuel of commitment.

Many have high ideals, gifted immensely yet never achieve more than a trivial view of success due to a lack of focus. Focus for the sake of simplicity is the ability to stay consistently engaged or to concentrate on something or someone. Focus is the fuel of commitment because nothing gets done without some form of focus.

> *Focus is the fuel of commitment.*

Henry Wadsworth's wise poetry is worth mentioning… "The heights by great men reached and kept, were not obtained by sudden flight, but they, while their companions slept, were toiling upward in the night." This is the problem; we sleep and become slothful because there is no fight in us. We are not hungry enough. In a marriage focus is necessary for the longevity and sustainability. It is easy to lose focus in a marriage. If one spouse becomes detached and alienated for whatever reason, this introduces a break in the relational continuity that is essential to stay engaged and for marriage to be fun. Will Smith and Jada Pinkett-Smith both say that creativity is essential in a marriage where you have to choose how happy you want to be in a marriage. That kind of marital bliss can only come through a committed focus from both parties.

9

THE IMPORTANCE OF FLIGHT INSTRUCTORS
THE ROLE OF MENTORS
You Cannot Learn to Fly By Yourself…
MARC GUEVARA

I believe that I do not necessarily have to make the same mistakes someone else made. Although, I have to admit that I have made some mistakes that some of my fore parents made. We have a cloud of witnesses that have gone before us to show us what works and what does not. Where the pitfalls are located ahead of us. Whether they are in personal relationships, business relationships, and political relationships.

In like manner, I can develop or innovate upon an existing idea or principle. Deep inside of us there is a well of creativity that most of us do not use or activate. It is said that we use up less than ten percent of our intellectual capacity. Yet we still make the same mistakes that our parents or those who have gone before us make. Even some businesses make the same mistakes in spite of the fact that there is enough empirical data to avoid them. For some ungodly reason, some of us do not fly higher than our genetically wired codes. Every man or woman has weaknesses. They range from addictions, bad habits, and mental strongholds, sexual, emotional and character based shortcomings. When we are faced with situations that challenge us in these areas, we naturally gravitate towards the easy way out, we press the default enter on our inner computer keyboard. Hollywood has depicted to us that it is okay to be a murderer, a thief, a rapist and greedy as long as you are a great actor. It is great for leading roles. But we have seen the ruin that follows these lifestyles.

Many individuals would have been much further along in their ventures and personal goals but simply do not listen to those who have more experience and knowledge of the past terrain. I am eternally grateful to those individuals who have helped to shape my thinking.

After I became a Christian as a young man,

I went back to my old ways rather rapidly until one day; a giant of a man named Roy Blyden came looking for me. He told me that I needed to grow in my conversion and of the necessity of mentoring in my new walk. He took time from his busy schedule to mentor me, teach me and finally he baptized me. But for Roy Blyden, I would not be writing this book. He became my friend and mentored me into the kingdom with solid principles that still guide me to this day. I will never forget him as long as I live.

Joshua Turnel Nelson was to me the greatest man that ever lived. He supervised and mentored me when I was a pioneering church founder in the Nederlands Antilles island of Curaçao. He taught me about discipline, the art of running for one's health, the necessity of fasting, and healthy eating habits. But for Turnel Nelson, I would not have been the man I am today. There is so much of what he taught me and the time I spent with him that still guides me today. I can still hear him chanting as we ran together,

"I love life, I love health,
For my health is my wealth."

Turnel Nelson ran like a young man. He ran effortlessly when he ran. I ran with him in Curaçao and even then I had trouble keeping up with him. He was also a spiritual giant who taught me how to glean immense revelation from the Bible. The running part was a key to his discipline and it became mine as well. He had no problem teaching me and sharing his inner wisdom as a father, a speaker and as a man. I am immensely grateful to his life and the legacy he left to me and many others.

Irvine Smith walked with me when I needed a path. He provided a template of what it means to serve others. He was more action than talk and he knew how to get things done. He was the epitome of transparency, humility and cool. I rarely ever saw him get angry. He was also the quintessential business-minded entrepreneur. I observed how he treated people and how he included me and others in the process so as to serve as a learning experience. As a leader he certainly spoke softly but always carried a big stick. He was my earliest mentor. A lot of Irvine Smith lives in me. A good mentor will influence your life, a great one will leave a piece of themselves with you for a lifetime.

Lastly but not the least, I would like to pay homage to a man who perhaps was one of the greatest men, who in my estimate ever walked upon the face of the earth in the 21st century. That man was David Wilkerson. He was the best mentor I ever had. I was very blessed to have walked with him for a very short time. During that time however, I saw the heart of a man who was selflessly benevolent, passionate about what he believed, humble in spirit, not given to excess, and sacrificial.

I saw how he was genuinely concerned for the poor, the downtrodden, the forgotten, those who were trapped by addictions, and unwed mothers. I experienced his caring manner first-hand. I saw him empty his wallet in my hands while I was a struggling college student who ministered with him in New York City. Pastor Dave as he was affectionately called was the best mentor I had. I have always striven to live a life that approximates those ideals.

Those who have scaled places we have never been, and overcame things we never overcome have invaluable wisdom to impart and deserve our focused attention. Succeeding at any venture is a journey. The notion of instant success and overnight sensations drives a lot of young people down a path of disappointment. All "self-made" millionaires had help. Every successful entrepreneur had a mentor. Be it something they read, something they heard, there is always the kernel of something that never existed somewhere. Many successful individuals are secretly unknown mentors for someone they do not even know. I encourage you to find a mentor, secretly or open. If they have written material, read them. If you have an opportunity to have an audience with them by all means pursue it.

10

DISCIPLINE

WHERE GROWTH BECOMES A SUSTAINABLE HABIT

The one who loves discipline loves knowledge, but the one who hates reproof is stupid.
PROVERBS 12:1

In keeping with the targeted premise of this book, I wanted to focus on an area that has stymied me and held many hostage. When I was in college, I was blessed to have had who I consider to be one of the best music theory teachers I ever had. He was a demure Chinese professor named Dr. David Nee To Sheng. Dr. Sheng and his wife Lydia were displaced persons from the Chinese war of the late 1940s when General Chiang Kai Sheik (also known as Jiang Jieshi) was in power.

Dr. Sheng had a very unique sense

of humor and used some of the strangest creative illustrations to teach some of his music theory principles. One morning, he came into class dressed with two different sets of shoes on his feet. He also had his shirt on backwards. The objective of his illustration though a bit extreme, was to illustrate the role of the key signature in music; either sharps or flats and how they are essential for driving the direction and tenor of a piece of music. Music must have directional structure he said and the key signature provided that.

Apart from that illustration and many others he made, Dr. Sheng had the most impact on my life as a young man in college. It started one day when he called me into his office. He took a personal interest in my academic as I was not doing too well in his theory class due to some distractions. He told me he had more expectations of me as a student and that I had more potential than I could imagine. He also told me that I needed to focus more on being a good student and less on the extra-curricular activities that I was too engaged in. At the time I was a cross-country runner and it was taking too much time away from my schoolwork. He pointedly said that I came to school to study and that should be my priority. Dr. Sheng told me in stern terms that I needed to buckle down and discipline myself to study. I cried in his office. His words resonated deeply within me because they identified problem areas in my life that no one had ever identified. He went the extra mile to help me discipline my life.

Over the next couple of years while in college, Dr. Sheng became my mentor. He saw an overnight change in my life after that initial encounter. He gave me some literature that has guided him as a young man called "Maxims for Living," which I still have to this day. I followed those steps and they served as the initial kernel to help me graduate a whole semester ahead of schedule.

The bulk of those maxims were about personal discipline. Personal discipline for our intents and purposes is the ability to bring your moral character, your desires and personal drive under control to achieve your desired goals. In other words you have an understanding of how to buffet or constrain your mind, body and spirit to avoid excess, distractions and, to refrain from letting your base desires take you off course. Personal discipline is important because the principles that govern or color one's ability to overcome or fall prey to personal weaknesses, run like a common thread in everything that you do. Personal discipline runs the gamut and spectrum of many areas of our lives. From overeating or gluttony, sexual indiscretions, slothfulness, time management, regular exercise, over spending, just to name a few are areas that need personal discipline.

If one lacks personal discipline, he or she runs the risk of living a life of personal self-imposed limits. You will be unable to run consistently and win, a life of hit and miss ensue, and success may only be marginal and short-lived. I have looked at the lives of many so-called successful CEOs of major corporations in the United States and Europe. They have been able to take corporations to great revenue heights but their personal lives were nothing like their successes.

Lack of personal disciplines brings shadows upon one's life. Bernie Madoff who made history with one of the largest Ponzi schemes in US history is spending the rest of this life in federal prison pondering a life of shadows. Every one of us is challenged by a different element. We are faced with a different enemy that wars within us. Be it greed, envy, lust or any other macabre desire, it is wise to bring your spirit under control so as to live a life of consistent integrity.

Left unchecked, a life that lacks personal discipline can ruin nations, corporations, churches and families. The lack of personal discipline manifests itself in many different ways in our current society. Hollywood would have us believe that excess in women is only a fad but lives are ruined in the process. CEOs of corporations would have us believe that as long as a company is profitable that it gives them license to destroy lives and act deceitfully in the market–place. Preachers would have us believe that as long as they have a large and successful church it gives them liberty to carry on with illicit relationships without regard for personal integrity and accountability.

Personal discipline is the most liberating character-building facet of human life. It allows one to build a life of trust that is fueled by consistently delivering at a high level. One is safe and comfortable within oneself by knowing that you do not have to look behind your back while walking in a public place. David Wilkerson, who lived a life of integrity like no other man I knew, was such a man. He was challenged like every other preacher but he refused to be caught up in the self-aggrandizement and wanton excess like other church leaders. He never drove a Bentley although he could have afforded one. Instead he chose to focus on the needs of the poor. He never sold his preachings although he could have easily commanded a pretty sum; instead he offered them freely as he had been given them.

It is not easy frankly to develop personal discipline. It is a life long pursuit. However, desire must precede its journey. Personal discipline can begin with easy steps such as desiring to improve your own health. It requires a daily deliberate regimen of doing something different every day to achieve a high level of personal health. Daily exercise, eating healthy, getting enough rest are some of the small steps one can do to achieve a semblance of a healthy lifestyle. Some people like to speed. It may behoove them to start leaving their point of origin earlier to avoid speeding. Speeding is not the problem but the lack of discipline is the culprit. Interestingly enough, however, people who are always late sometimes have a habit of speeding because the discipline of proper time management is not in place and it runs like a common thread in everything they do. The same principle applies to every bad habit we have.

Those who have problems with overeating may need additional professional help but the desire to change your life must precipitate the change first. Ask yourself if you want to live a short life. The statistics do not lie. Overweight people statistically life a shorter life than most people with healthy body to height ratios. Addictions are terrible and life controlling, so I know that personal discipline is not easy but others have done it and you are not alone. I once knew a young man named Miguel (name changed to protect individuals). He was an amazing young speaker, charismatic, a real people person but Miguel had a dark passion that controlled him. He had trouble controlling his sexual desires. He, like many who suffer in silence, paid no attention to this area and continued throughout his life to ignore this life controlling problem. He was married, had children, was highly respected but he could climb no higher than his ability to overcome that life controlling problem. He eventually abandoned his desire from becoming a speaker, started drinking and using drugs. His family life fell apart and did not fare too well financially. He died about seven years ago, alone in his apartment from a massive heart attack. The moral of this story should not fly by glibly. Life is a morass of decisions and choices that become a lifestyle and eventually a destiny.

To achieve sustainable success at anything you must ask yourself what kind of life do I want to live consistently and take *intentional* and *deliberate* steps to change the rhythm and direction of your life. To go beyond where you are requires mentors, a massive change in your thinking, less ego trips and difficult decisions to put your life on a sustainability trajectory. While I subscribe to the model that changing our thinking serves as a catalyst to the beginning of real change, it is new fresh knowledge, new experiences, new mentors, that feed the way we think first and encourages creative thinking. This demonstrably will usher in a path of discovery that will eclipse anything else. No one can continue to do the same thing over and over again and get new results. It is just pure madness.

Our society has gotten so narcissistic as we

are so stricken with Hollywood and its cultural offsprings. You as an individual cannot have real and meaningful success until you make a real and meaningful difference in the lives of others. Because at the end of the day, just as people do not always remember what you said or do, they invariably remember how you made them feel. Then and only then can you really fly?

NOTES

ABOUT THE AUTHOR

Marc Guevara is a raconteur, author, publisher and entrepreneur. Mr. Guevara has spent several years as a technology architect in the Silicon Valley area. He is a graduate of Nyack College, New York and holds an MBA from Walden University, Minneapolis, Minnesota.

He lives in Tampa, Florida with his wife, Dr. Beverly Hernandez, and their two children.

Marc Guevara is available for select readings, lectures and story telling. To inquire about appearances kindly contact the Digital Artery Media Group Publishers at marc@damgrp.com.

ABOUT THE MAIN TYPEFACE

A dutch typographer named William Caslon designed the original typeface "Caslon" from which the Adobe Caslon Pro typeface was derived and is primarily used in the content of this book. It was chosen for its simplicity, its picturesque way of sitting on a page, delicate lines and visual eloquence. As an early designer and publisher of printed materials, William Caslon, worked circa 1720–1766 and based his type on Dutch models.

ENDNOTES

1. Kairos: Kairos is an ancient Greek word meaning the "right or opportune moment"
2. From "The Life of Albert Einstein"
3. Bishop Tudor Bismarck speaking at New Birth Missionary Baptist Church, November 14th, 2004
4. Dr. John Maxwell "The 21 Irrefutable Laws of Leadership"
5. King James Bible...Matthew 6:
6. Bennis and Nanus et al, "Transformational Leaders"
7. Franky Schaffer, "Addicted to Mediocrity"
8. Bennis and Nanus et al, "Transformational Leaders"

9. Possibility Thinkers, Robert S. Shuller
10. King James Bible 1 Peter
11. Dr. John Maxwell, "The 21 Irrefutable Laws of Leadership,"
12. Benjamin Franklin
13. Dr. John Maxwell, "Talent is not Enough"
14. Helicar, a futuristic flying vehicle
15. http://www.netflix.com
16. The Leader of the Future: New Visions, Strategies, and Practices for the Next Era by Richard Beckhard, Frances Hesselbein, Marshall Goldsmith

NOTES

NOTES